Arched Eyebrows

a chapbook

David Appelbaum

ISBN: 978-81-19654-27-7

First Edition: 2024
Rs. 200/-

Cyberwit.net
HIG 45 Kaushambi Kunj, Kalindipuram
Allahabad - 211011 (U.P.) India
http://www.cyberwit.net
Tel: +(91) 9415091004
E-mail: info@cyberwit.net

Printed at Repro India Limited.

Dedication

To Amiya Chakravarty

Contents

Haul

the long winding road
in dreams

escapes a globetrotter's
cool enthusiasm

I'm the winch
trying to hoist

into the next stanza
with right intent

cranking the rotor
to uncurl verbs

so to know precisely
what I'm to drop—

to bury feeling
under these words

then rise from
bed in good graces

nothing dangling

Perspective

‘the sun looked
down on fields of grain’

can it see
light that is invisible?

to factor out
effects

of one’s own
guilt and kin

real things
leave shadows

a vale of stories
that makes credible

even the life
of dung beetles

this is joy

Advertising

watermelon without seeds:
a new nature meme

like decaffeinated coffee
or sugarless candy

points toward pleasure
stripped of cost—

which is cultivated
melancholy

like a day-glow sign
on a shiny Ford truck

Mobile Appearance
Restoration Service

men are from Mars

Sales pitch

a fire extinguisher
on the museum wall
wasn't part of any exhibit

but nobody knew

. . .

our inner-most feelings
are often disguised—
take homespun gestures

like scratching one's head

. . .

on a white board
you draw an ellipse
an infinity cupped

under a bleeding heart

. . .

the inaudible light
wires itself
for full spectrum sound

'now available in your area'

Ceremony

a very faint smell
of varnish

with droning
crickets in rose bushes

reminds me of our *chado*
grinding green tea

into a giddy frizz
small round leaves

on an onyx board
lacquered exquisitely thin

each brush stroke
drops hints

that cause the rim
to blanch

it might be a poem

The slow march

daisy after motherwort
after pimpernel

it's a play
with flimsy petals
to keep time

as if 'open'
'close'; were sounds
of a mantra

to unleash
the hours, sparing
a few mauve leaves

when did you first
know the nirvana
of color

was meant for you?
when did you
forget?

The call

a bird whistle
is from a bird

silver tinting
these reflexive stanzas

that have an ear
for pitch

a flush of notes
trails like lookalikes

morning poured
from a flute

into the columbarium
of my brain

between there and next
a reverb bounces

happy
not immortal

Romance

lost gloves
sewn to a wicker basket

await someone's hand
to grasp flatten

smooth stretch
after a friendly

pat
and faint hesitancy

insert with care
forefinger to

forefinger pinky
to pinky

and ah, closure
is a good fit—

when you do that
I want you

to hug me too

The cap

a ripe tomato wears
a crown of gauzy white mold

something is going around

referring to special ills
that implicate you

the passage signified—
senescence—

you don't get it
until you have it

(always pre-owned)

arisen effortlessly
without sensation

the mind 's wild haunt
splits as you look

red crowing yellow seeds

it's your story of
personal existence

but really the fact is
summer heat drives mildew

Without music

a storm left the sky
orange as a life
preserver

with a single contrail
to tie it
around my waist

but when I ducked down
to pull it over
my head

water plugged my ears
my voice called out

'Enough. No, *more*.'

Multiple personalities

yellow leaves
stepping stones
across tarmac

in a millipede's eyes
continents adrift

with persistent desire
larboard
at first frost's

prophecies
of grey death

while I
in the first person
stand stock-still

believing myself
a butterfly
trapped in my flesh

unable to take
the risky step

toward flight

Picayune

now the world is different

our incensed vigil
over name-changes

even the smallest
most under-rated

like dots of an ‘i’
or a ‘j’

is an endangered species

each and every tittle
reminds us of something

like our lack of
real depth-of-being

Nerves

topsy turvy

the given knows
your refusal

since greed
is law
desire brays

it's dumb to be
gifted

meaning, too easy
on yourself

tired of negating
the no

relax, bend down
look between your legs—

the sun also rises
bigger than ever

seen downside up
upside down

Twice

the irony of mirrors
doubles everything

things of two suns
two moons

twin loves twin
hates twin

approving thoughts
are twice as many
as before

but 'before' also has
a Siamese
in time

new math
but to be invested

to get a handle
on the menagerie

to halve things
heal double vision

scratch second sight

forget two heads
are better than

one

Boxed in

to fill a blank
under the nib

script's well-being
in feeling out
an environment

words have to
have clout to

catch us where
we are today

right or wrong
free or stuck

which is why
I like photons'

simple ergs of
energy

The call

no space to install
a new

novelty whose premise

to un-pump desire
does nothing

at the gas station
a man, shaggy white hair

above a jean jacket,
plops cans from the trash

into a black plastic bag
over one shoulder—

shushing thin metal

angelic voices

Autumn

a blush comes from
the faint lift
arched eyebrows
rolling eyes

a soubrette
sentimental cruelty

but a pink-lined
oak leaf

has bright chemicals
that return love

from enzymes
in flush of need

bounded desire is
a snare that
leaves us thinking

consciousness
is so boring

let's just rake

Medley

'must win'
sign on heaven's gate

meet those elected
new souls

as backwash of
revelation

hear seraphim cheep
reserve space

. . . . .

triumph is
synonymous with
increased

input
influence is
God

. . . . .

necessity mothers
parsing

leaves
littering the lawn

each feeling
obedient to loll

. . . . .

belief is a loss
we suffer

when seeming flees

Care-giving

a lone house wren
does its pensum
under a plastic feeder

afterthought:
refuse to absolve

hunger, its clairvoyance
teases
to cast out devils

of hope

since I have extra seed

for a pair of mourning doves
on a high-rise branch—
study of patience

as in thinking
everything sparkles
and then doesn't

Reproduction

small brown spider
pushes egg sac
up a windowpane

outside: her aim
to be the sun

put winter on ice

she's part way up
speaking of herself
to herself

arachnid phonemes
fall like skips

a refrain
to herself
for scheming

light
she utters speech

like altitude

it's the weave
a god would knit

Afterlife

does the sun really
have rays (radii)

above us behind us
eternally to fret

in glints we can't
conceive

glancing off
the face of delight

like a Farmers' Almanac
sketch

warming chilling freezing
a barren house

where the soul was believed
to live

and go 'where'?

The news

endgame for imaging
Rover lands on Mars

rock looks like rock

it was our understanding
that things would be
stippled

faded

the way nostalgia works
a honeycomb of canals

plied by bogeymen
in Venetian hats

but no, there next to it
lolling on the horizon

an ancient Coca-Cola truck

www.ingramcontent.com/pod-product-compliance
Lightning Source LLC
Chambersburg PA
CBHW022205160726
48282CB00024B/327